# NO MORE PEANUTS BOOK 2: HOW TO EARN MORE MONEY

# No More Peanuts Book 2: How to Earn More Money

Walter the Educator

Silent King Books
A WhichHead Entertainment Imprint

Copyright © 2024 by Walter the Educator

All rights reserved. No part of this book may be reproduced in any manner whatsoever without written permission except in the case of brief quotations embodied in critical articles and reviews.

First Printing, 2024

Disclaimer

The author and publisher offer this information without warranties expressed or implied. No matter the grounds, neither the author nor the publisher will be accountable for any losses, injuries, or other damages caused by the reader's use of this book. Your use of this book acknowledges an understanding and acceptance of this disclaimer.

No More Peanuts Book 2: How to Earn More Money is a little problem-solver book by Walter the Educator that belongs to the Little Problem Solver Books Series. Collect them all and more books at WaltertheEducator.com

# LITTLE PROBLEM
# SOLVER BOOKS

# INTRO

Earning more money is a goal that resonates universally. Whether you're looking to increase your income to improve your standard of living, achieve financial independence, or fund specific dreams and aspirations, there are countless ways to achieve this objective. This essay explores the strategies for earning more money, from traditional employment and entrepreneurship to passive income streams, investment opportunities, and the role of skills development.

# 1. Understanding the Foundations of Earning More Money

*The Role of Mindset*

Before embarking on any journey to increase earnings, it is essential to adopt the right mindset. A growth mindset, believing that your abilities and intelligence can be developed, lays the groundwork for success. People with a fixed mindset often perceive financial growth as limited by external factors, whereas a growth-oriented perspective focuses on opportunities and solutions.

For where two or three
are gathered together in my name,
there am I in the midst of them
- Matthew 18:20

Reiterate
THIS PHRASE
"I Will Earn More Money"

## FREE

DOWNLOAD AND ACCESS THE HIT SONG
"NO MORE PEANUTS"
WaltertheEducator.com/NoMorePeanuts.html

*Assessing Your Current Financial Standing*

An honest evaluation of your current income, expenses, and financial goals is critical. This assessment helps identify areas where you can cut costs, allocate resources more efficiently, or redirect efforts to boost earnings.

For where two or three
are gathered together in my name,
there am I in the midst of them
- Matthew 18:20

## Reiterate
## THIS PHRASE
## "I Will Earn More Money"

## <u>FREE</u>

DOWNLOAD AND ACCESS THE HIT SONG
"NO MORE PEANUTS"
WaltertheEducator.com/NoMorePeanuts.html

## 2. Leveraging Traditional Employment

*Enhancing Your Current Career*

If you are employed, increasing your income often starts with maximizing your value in your current role:

- **Skill Development**: Continuously improving your expertise through courses, certifications, and professional development makes you a more valuable employee. Advanced skills in technology, management, or specialized fields can lead to promotions and salary increases.

For where two or three
are gathered together in my name,
there am I in the midst of them
- Matthew 18:20

Reiterate
THIS PHRASE
"I Will Earn More Money"

FREE

DOWNLOAD AND ACCESS THE HIT SONG
"NO MORE PEANUTS"
WaltertheEducator.com/NoMorePeanuts.html

- **Networking**: Building relationships within and beyond your organization can uncover hidden opportunities, such as new roles, projects, or mentorships.

For where two or three
are gathered together in my name,
there am I in the midst of them
- Matthew 18:20

# Reiterate
# THIS PHRASE
# "I Will Earn More Money"

## **FREE**

DOWNLOAD AND ACCESS THE HIT SONG
"NO MORE PEANUTS"
WaltertheEducator.com/NoMorePeanuts.html

- **Negotiating Salary**: Many people hesitate to ask for raises, but negotiating your pay based on performance and market benchmarks is a vital skill.

For where two or three
are gathered together in my name,
there am I in the midst of them
- Matthew 18:20

## Reiterate
## THIS PHRASE
## "I Will Earn More Money"

## FREE

DOWNLOAD AND ACCESS THE HIT SONG
"NO MORE PEANUTS"
WaltertheEducator.com/NoMorePeanuts.html

*Switching Careers or Industries*

Sometimes, the key to earning more lies in changing industries or pursuing high-demand roles. For example:

- Careers in technology, healthcare, and finance often offer competitive salaries.

For where two or three
are gathered together in my name,
there am I in the midst of them
- Matthew 18:20

# Reiterate
# THIS PHRASE
# "I Will Earn More Money"

## FREE

DOWNLOAD AND ACCESS THE HIT SONG
"NO MORE PEANUTS"
WaltertheEducator.com/NoMorePeanuts.html

- Transitioning into roles such as software development, data analysis, or digital marketing may require additional training but can result in significant income growth.

For where two or three
are gathered together in my name,
there am I in the midst of them
- Matthew 18:20

## Reiterate
## THIS PHRASE
## "I Will Earn More Money"

## <u>FREE</u>

DOWNLOAD AND ACCESS THE HIT SONG
"NO MORE PEANUTS"
WaltertheEducator.com/NoMorePeanuts.html

## 3. Exploring Entrepreneurship

*Starting a Business*

Entrepreneurship is a proven avenue for earning more money, albeit one that requires careful planning, persistence, and adaptability. Here's how to approach it:

- **Identify a Niche**: Successful businesses often cater to specific, underserved markets. Identifying a gap in the market can set your business apart.

For where two or three
are gathered together in my name,
there am I in the midst of them
- Matthew 18:20

# Reiterate
# THIS PHRASE
# "I Will Earn More Money"

## FREE

DOWNLOAD AND ACCESS THE HIT SONG
"NO MORE PEANUTS"
WaltertheEducator.com/NoMorePeanuts.html

- **Low-Cost Startups**: Many businesses, especially online, require minimal upfront investment. Dropshipping, content creation, and freelancing are examples.

For where two or three
are gathered together in my name,
there am I in the midst of them
- Matthew 18:20

## Reiterate
## THIS PHRASE
## "I Will Earn More Money"

## FREE

DOWNLOAD AND ACCESS THE HIT SONG
"NO MORE PEANUTS"
WaltertheEducator.com/NoMorePeanuts.html

- **Scalability**: Focus on business ideas that can scale, meaning your revenue potential is not tied to your hours worked.

For where two or three
are gathered together in my name,
there am I in the midst of them
- Matthew 18:20

# Reiterate
# THIS PHRASE
# "I Will Earn More Money"

## FREE

DOWNLOAD AND ACCESS THE HIT SONG
"NO MORE PEANUTS"
WaltertheEducator.com/NoMorePeanuts.html

*Side Hustles*

Side hustles are flexible ways to supplement your primary income. Popular side hustles include:

- Freelance writing, graphic design, or consulting.
- Ride-sharing, food delivery, or other gig-economy opportunities.
- Selling products on platforms like Etsy, Amazon, or eBay.

For where two or three
are gathered together in my name,
there am I in the midst of them
- Matthew 18:20

## Reiterate
## THIS PHRASE
## "I Will Earn More Money"

## FREE

DOWNLOAD AND ACCESS THE HIT SONG
"NO MORE PEANUTS"
WaltertheEducator.com/NoMorePeanuts.html

## 4. Building Passive Income Streams

Passive income is money earned with minimal active effort after an initial investment of time or resources. Developing passive income streams can significantly boost long-term financial stability.

For where two or three
are gathered together in my name,
there am I in the midst of them
- Matthew 18:20

Reiterate
THIS PHRASE
"I Will Earn More Money"

## FREE

DOWNLOAD AND ACCESS THE HIT SONG
"NO MORE PEANUTS"
WaltertheEducator.com/NoMorePeanuts.html

*Real Estate Investments*

Owning rental properties is a traditional but effective way to earn passive income. Options include:

- Purchasing and renting out residential or commercial properties.

For where two or three
are gathered together in my name,
there am I in the midst of them
- Matthew 18:20

## Reiterate
## THIS PHRASE
## "I Will Earn More Money"

## FREE

DOWNLOAD AND ACCESS THE HIT SONG
"NO MORE PEANUTS"
WaltertheEducator.com/NoMorePeanuts.html

- Investing in Real Estate Investment Trusts (REITs), which allow you to invest in real estate without owning physical property.

*Dividend Stocks*

Dividend-paying stocks provide regular payouts to shareholders, offering a steady income stream. Investing in established companies with a history of dividend payouts is often a low-risk way to grow wealth.

For where two or three
are gathered together in my name,
there am I in the midst of them
- Matthew 18:20

## Reiterate
## THIS PHRASE
## "I Will Earn More Money"

## FREE

DOWNLOAD AND ACCESS THE HIT SONG
"NO MORE PEANUTS"
WaltertheEducator.com/NoMorePeanuts.html

*Digital Products and Royalties*

Creating digital products such as e-books, online courses, or software tools can generate recurring income. Once developed, these products can be sold repeatedly with little additional effort.

For where two or three
are gathered together in my name,
there am I in the midst of them
- Matthew 18:20

Reiterate
THIS PHRASE
"I Will Earn More Money"

## FREE

DOWNLOAD AND ACCESS THE HIT SONG
"NO MORE PEANUTS"
WaltertheEducator.com/NoMorePeanuts.html

## 5. Leveraging Investments

Investing is a cornerstone of financial growth. By putting your money to work, you can generate returns that outpace inflation and compound over time.

For where two or three
are gathered together in my name,
there am I in the midst of them
- Matthew 18:20

Reiterate
THIS PHRASE
"I Will Earn More Money"

## FREE

DOWNLOAD AND ACCESS THE HIT SONG
"NO MORE PEANUTS"
WaltertheEducator.com/NoMorePeanuts.html

*Stocks and Bonds*

- **Stocks**: Investing in companies allows you to benefit from their growth. Stock portfolios can be diversified across industries and regions for risk management.
  - **Bonds**: Bonds are fixed-income securities that provide steady returns. They are considered safer than stocks but typically offer lower yields.

For where two or three
are gathered together in my name,
there am I in the midst of them
- Matthew 18:20

## Reiterate
## THIS PHRASE
## "I Will Earn More Money"

## FREE

DOWNLOAD AND ACCESS THE HIT SONG
"NO MORE PEANUTS"
WaltertheEducator.com/NoMorePeanuts.html

*Mutual Funds and ETFs*

For those new to investing, mutual funds and Exchange-Traded Funds (ETFs) offer diversified portfolios managed by professionals. These funds spread your investment across multiple assets, reducing risk.

For where two or three
are gathered together in my name,
there am I in the midst of them
- Matthew 18:20

Reiterate
THIS PHRASE
"I Will Earn More Money"

**FREE**

DOWNLOAD AND ACCESS THE HIT SONG
"NO MORE PEANUTS"
WaltertheEducator.com/NoMorePeanuts.html

*Cryptocurrency and Alternative Investments*

Cryptocurrency, while volatile, has gained popularity as a high-risk, high-reward investment. Alternative investments like gold, art, or collectibles can also diversify your portfolio.

For where two or three
are gathered together in my name,
there am I in the midst of them
- Matthew 18:20

Reiterate
THIS PHRASE
"I Will Earn More Money"

## FREE

DOWNLOAD AND ACCESS THE HIT SONG
"NO MORE PEANUTS"
WaltertheEducator.com/NoMorePeanuts.html

### 6. Upskilling and Education

*Acquiring High-Income Skills*

Certain skills consistently command high salaries in the job market. Examples include:

- **Tech Skills**: Programming, cybersecurity, and AI development.

> For where two or three
> are gathered together in my name,
> there am I in the midst of them
> - Matthew 18:20

# Reiterate
# THIS PHRASE
# "I Will Earn More Money"

## FREE

DOWNLOAD AND ACCESS THE HIT SONG
"NO MORE PEANUTS"
WaltertheEducator.com/NoMorePeanuts.htm

-

- **Management Skills**: Project management, leadership, and strategic planning.

For where two or three
are gathered together in my name,
there am I in the midst of them
- Matthew 18:20

# Reiterate
# THIS PHRASE
# "I Will Earn More Money"

## FREE

DOWNLOAD AND ACCESS THE HIT SONG
"NO MORE PEANUTS"
WaltertheEducator.com/NoMorePeanuts.html

- **Creative Skills**: Content creation, graphic design, and video production.

For where two or three
are gathered together in my name,
there am I in the midst of them
- Matthew 18:20

# Reiterate
# THIS PHRASE
# "I Will Earn More Money"

## <u>FREE</u>

DOWNLOAD AND ACCESS THE HIT SONG
"NO MORE PEANUTS"
WaltertheEducator.com/NoMorePeanuts.html

*Continuous Learning*

The rapid pace of technological and economic change necessitates lifelong learning. Online platforms like Coursera, Udemy, and LinkedIn Learning provide affordable courses to enhance your expertise.

For where two or three
are gathered together in my name,
there am I in the midst of them
- Matthew 18:20

Reiterate
THIS PHRASE
"I Will Earn More Money"

## FREE

DOWNLOAD AND ACCESS THE HIT SONG
"NO MORE PEANUTS"
WaltertheEducator.com/NoMorePeanuts.html

## 7. Managing and Maximizing Time

Time management is directly tied to income generation. Efficiently allocating your time can help you achieve more in less time.

For where two or three
are gathered together in my name,
there am I in the midst of them
- Matthew 18:20

Reiterate
THIS PHRASE
"I Will Earn More Money"

## FREE

DOWNLOAD AND ACCESS THE HIT SONG
"NO MORE PEANUTS"
WaltertheEducator.com/NoMorePeanuts.html

*Prioritizing High-Value Activities*

Focus on tasks that generate the most significant results, whether in your job, business, or side hustle. Outsourcing or automating low-value activities can free up time for strategic efforts.

For where two or three
are gathered together in my name,
there am I in the midst of them
- Matthew 18:20

## Reiterate
## THIS PHRASE
## "I Will Earn More Money"

## FREE

DOWNLOAD AND ACCESS THE HIT SONG
"NO MORE PEANUTS"
WaltertheEducator.com/NoMorePeanuts.html

*Embracing the Power of Routine*

A structured daily routine improves productivity. Incorporating habits like goal setting, task prioritization, and regular breaks ensures consistent progress toward earning more money.

For where two or three
are gathered together in my name,
there am I in the midst of them
- Matthew 18:20

## Reiterate
## THIS PHRASE
## "I Will Earn More Money"

## FREE

DOWNLOAD AND ACCESS THE HIT SONG
"NO MORE PEANUTS"
WaltertheEducator.com/NoMorePeanuts.html

## 8. Embracing Technology and Automation

*Online Platforms*

The internet has opened up countless earning opportunities:

- **Freelance Marketplaces**: Platforms like Upwork and Fiverr connect freelancers with clients worldwide.
  - **E-commerce**: Websites like Shopify allow entrepreneurs to sell products globally.

For where two or three
are gathered together in my name,
there am I in the midst of them
- Matthew 18:20

# Reiterate
# THIS PHRASE
# "I Will Earn More Money"

# <u>FREE</u>

DOWNLOAD AND ACCESS THE HIT SONG
"NO MORE PEANUTS"
WaltertheEducator.com/NoMorePeanuts.html

- **Social Media Monetization**: Creators can earn through ad revenue, sponsorships, and affiliate marketing.

*Automation Tools*

Automating repetitive tasks in business or personal finance, such as billing or social media scheduling, increases efficiency and scalability.

For where two or three
are gathered together in my name,
there am I in the midst of them
- Matthew 18:20

## Reiterate
## THIS PHRASE
## "I Will Earn More Money"

## FREE

DOWNLOAD AND ACCESS THE HIT SONG
"NO MORE PEANUTS"
WaltertheEducator.com/NoMorePeanuts.html

## 9. Developing Multiple Income Streams

Relying on a single source of income is risky. Diversifying your income ensures financial security and flexibility.

*Part-Time Opportunities*

Taking on a part-time job in addition to your main role can boost your earnings. Teaching, tutoring, or working in retail are common options.

For where two or three
are gathered together in my name,
there am I in the midst of them
- Matthew 18:20

# Reiterate
# THIS PHRASE
# "I Will Earn More Money"

## FREE

DOWNLOAD AND ACCESS THE HIT SONG
"NO MORE PEANUTS"
WaltertheEducator.com/NoMorePeanuts.html

*Freelancing*

Freelancers have the freedom to take on multiple clients and projects simultaneously. This flexibility often results in higher overall income.

For where two or three
are gathered together in my name,
there am I in the midst of them
- Matthew 18:20

## Reiterate
## THIS PHRASE
## "I Will Earn More Money"

## <u>FREE</u>

DOWNLOAD AND ACCESS THE HIT SONG
"NO MORE PEANUTS"
WaltertheEducator.com/NoMorePeanuts.html

## 10. Practicing Smart Financial Habits

*Budgeting and Saving*

A solid financial foundation requires careful budgeting:

- Allocate a portion of your income toward savings and investments.
- Use apps to track expenses and identify areas for improvement.

For where two or three
are gathered together in my name,
there am I in the midst of them
- Matthew 18:20

Reiterate
THIS PHRASE
"I Will Earn More Money"

## FREE

DOWNLOAD AND ACCESS THE HIT SONG
"NO MORE PEANUTS"
WaltertheEducator.com/NoMorePeanuts.html

*Avoiding Debt*

High-interest debt erodes wealth. Paying off credit cards and loans promptly prevents unnecessary financial strain.

*Reinvesting Earnings*

Reinvesting a portion of your income into skill development, business expansion, or investments accelerates growth.

For where two or three
are gathered together in my name,
there am I in the midst of them
- Matthew 18:20

## Reiterate
## THIS PHRASE
## "I Will Earn More Money"

## FREE

DOWNLOAD AND ACCESS THE HIT SONG
"NO MORE PEANUTS"
WaltertheEducator.com/NoMorePeanuts.html

## 11. Building a Personal Brand

In today's digital age, personal branding is a powerful tool for increasing income potential. Your online presence, expertise, and reputation can lead to new opportunities.

For where two or three
are gathered together in my name,
there am I in the midst of them
- Matthew 18:20

Reiterate
THIS PHRASE
"I Will Earn More Money"

## FREE

DOWNLOAD AND ACCESS THE HIT SONG
"NO MORE PEANUTS"
WaltertheEducator.com/NoMorePeanuts.html

*Establishing Expertise*

Create and share valuable content through blogs, videos, or social media. Demonstrating expertise in your field builds credibility and attracts clients or employers.

*Networking*

Connecting with industry peers, influencers, and potential clients expands your reach and opens doors to lucrative opportunities.

For where two or three
are gathered together in my name,
there am I in the midst of them
- Matthew 18:20

## Reiterate THIS PHRASE "I Will Earn More Money"

## FREE

DOWNLOAD AND ACCESS THE HIT SONG
"NO MORE PEANUTS"
WaltertheEducator.com/NoMorePeanuts.html

## 12. Overcoming Challenges

The journey to earning more money is not without obstacles. Common challenges include:

- **Fear of Failure**: Overcome this by setting small, achievable goals.

For where two or three
are gathered together in my name,
there am I in the midst of them
- Matthew 18:20

# Reiterate
# THIS PHRASE
# "I Will Earn More Money"

## <u>FREE</u>

DOWNLOAD AND ACCESS THE HIT SONG
"NO MORE PEANUTS"
WaltertheEducator.com/NoMorePeanuts.html

- **Lack of Knowledge**: Address this through education and mentorship.

For where two or three
are gathered together in my name,
there am I in the midst of them
- Matthew 18:20

# Reiterate
# THIS PHRASE
# "I Will Earn More Money"

## FREE

DOWNLOAD AND ACCESS THE HIT SONG
"NO MORE PEANUTS"
WaltertheEducator.com/NoMorePeanuts.html

- **Limited Resources**: Start small and scale up as you gain experience and capital.

For where two or three
are gathered together in my name,
there am I in the midst of them
- Matthew 18:20

## Reiterate
## THIS PHRASE
## "I Will Earn More Money"

## FREE

DOWNLOAD AND ACCESS THE HIT SONG
"NO MORE PEANUTS"
WaltertheEducator.com/NoMorePeanuts.html

## Conclusion

Earning more money requires a blend of strategic planning, consistent effort, and adaptability. By leveraging traditional employment, entrepreneurship, passive income, and smart financial habits, anyone can increase their earnings and achieve their financial goals. Whether through enhancing your skills, investing wisely, or embracing innovation, the possibilities for financial growth are virtually limitless. Remember, the journey to wealth begins with a single step, take that step today and commit to a future of prosperity.

# ABOUT THE CREATOR

Walter the Educator is one of the pseudonyms for Walter Anderson. Formally educated in Chemistry, Business, and Education, he is an educator, an author, a diverse entrepreneur, and he is the son of a disabled war veteran. "Walter the Educator" shares his time between educating and creating. He holds interests and owns several creative projects that entertain, enlighten, enhance, and educate, hoping to inspire and motivate you. Follow, find new works, and stay up to date with Walter the Educator™

at WaltertheEducator.com